Teach Yourself To Play Bass

MORTY MANUS & RON MANUS

Alfred Music
P.O. Box 10003
Van Nuys, CA 91410-0003
alfred.com

Book & DVD
ISBN-10: 1-4706-2601-2
ISBN-13: 978-1-4706-2601-3

GETTING STARTED A SHORT HISTORY OF THE BASS GUITAR

The bass line as we know it can be traced back hundreds of years. For example, in the music of J.S. Bach (1685–1750), the bass line is as important as the soprano, alto, and tenor parts. In classical orchestral music, the bass line is played by the upright bass, or bass violas as it was originally called. In early forms of African-American music, such as ragtime and New Orleans jazz, the bass line was played by a brass bass or tuba. Because of breathing requirements, the tuba played a basic two-beats-to-the-bar rhythm. This gave early jazz and dance music an oom-pah feel. As jazz evolved into the era of swing (about 1935), musical compositions became more complex, and in the works of jazz greats such as Duke Ellington, Count Basie and Benny Goodman, a four-beats-to-the-bar feel began to predominate. Since the brass bass was incapable of playing this rhythm, the acoustic, upright bass took over the bass line.

However, the acoustic bass had its own limitations. It could not produce a large enough sound to be heard over the big bands of the period (often seven brass, five reeds, piano, guitar, and drums). The acoustic bass is also very large and quite difficult to transport. These were the problems that plagued bass players until the invention of the electric bass guitar.

The modern electric bass guitar was invented by Clarence Leo Fender. In 1951, the Fender Musical Instrument Company introduced the Fender Precision Bass. Leo Fender had set out to invent the electric bass guitar specifically to solve the low volume and large size problems of the upright bass. He called his invention the Precision Bass because by adding frets to the fingerboard, the problem of playing out of tune was also solved. The original Precision Bass was modeled after the Fender Broadcaster guitar, first introduced in 1948. Although the original design was slightly modified over the years, the Precision bass has remained basically the same to this day.

Today, there are many companies building basses. Their size, shapes, and sounds vary. There are some basses with five, six, or even more strings. Even with all these innovations, the standard four-string bass is the most common choice of bassists.

 **THE BASS GUITAR**

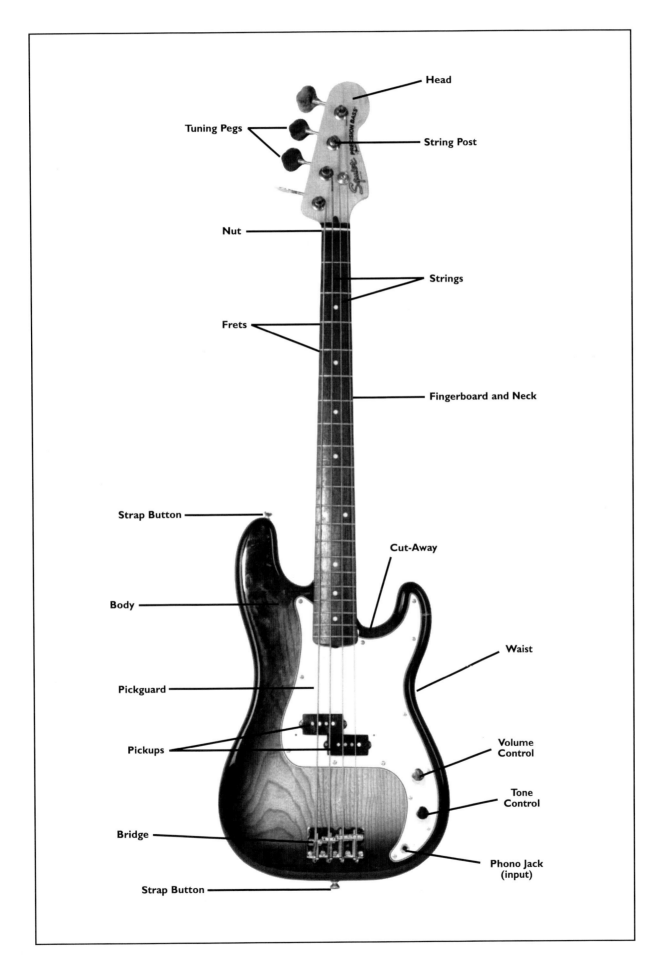

BUYING A BASS GUITAR

The most important thing to remember when buying an electric bass guitar is whether you'll be comfortable playing this instrument for years to come. Many bass players have made the mistake of buying a bass because of its looks, its brand name or because their favorite bass player uses that model. Later they find out that it has become uncomfortable to use. Maybe it's too heavy to hold for a long while, or perhaps the neck doesn't feel right under their hand. This can be a costly mistake and can prevent a beginning musician from progressing.

Other players prefer a brand new, shiny, right-off-the-assembly-line bass. Your local music store is the easiest place to find a new instrument. Your two main choices when purchasing a new bass guitar are either factory or custom built. Fender, Gibson, Peavey, Rickenbacker, Ibanez, Yamaha, and Schecter are some of the most commonly found factory built basses available. Whichever you choose, the main thing to take into account is price. Most new factory made basses cost between $500 and $1,000; custom-made instruments can cost upwards of $2,000 and above.

New or Used?
Whether you decide to buy a new or used bass, there are several important things to remember:

1. Whenever possible, bring along an experienced bass player (or even a guitar player) when purchasing your bass. A knowledgeable musician will be able to spot things that you might miss.

2. Check the condition of the instrument very carefully. It doesn't matter whether you're buying a brand new Fender Precision or a 1957 classic, check the following items:

The Neck
This is the single most important thing on any stringed instrument. Look for bowing or warping. Bass strings, when fully wound, exert a tremendous pull on the neck and can cause it to bow (like an archery bow). Also, the thicker strings exert more pull than the thinner ones leading to warping (side-to-side bending of the neck). Look down the neck lengthwise, either from the head down or the body up. Make sure the neck is straight, not arched or bent, and that the frets are in a straight line without one side or the other being higher in places. If everything looks "straight as an arrow," then it's O.K.

Hardware
Make sure the tuning pegs turn smoothly and evenly. Loose pegs (with play in them) are no good. They will slip and go out of tune. Check the bridge to make sure it's in good working order and that there are no missing pieces. Also, make sure the bridge is securely attached to the body of the bass.

Electronics
You can't check the electronics without plugging the bass into an amp. Turn the volume on the bass all the way up (the amp doesn't have to be that loud) and listen closely for any humming or buzzing sounds coming from the bass. Turn both the volume and tone knobs back and forth a few times to be sure there aren't a lot of crackling noises coming from them. If the bass has more than one pickup and has a pickup select switch, check each pickup individually. Also,

check any other knobs or switches the same way. Any type of noise or interference can mean that the electronics need repair. This is not necessarily a reason for rejecting the instrument, but you should get an estimate from a qualified repair man before agreeing to a purchase price.

Overall Condition
A new instrument should be spotless, without scratches or nicks. The condition of used basses will vary greatly. Don't worry about scratches or dents on the body of a used bass, especially on the back, it won't affect the quality of the sound. However, beware of any damage to the neck, head, and any vital mechanical or electronic parts.

Cases
Always get a case. New basses should always come with a good hard shell case (not cardboard). If a used bass doesn't have a case, check its condition with extra care and buy a case for it as soon as possible.

Amplifiers
There are as many different amps available as there are basses. Obviously, the Fender Company was one of the first to produce an amp specifically designed for bass players. Some other well-known amplifier manufacturers are Ampeg, Peavey and Hartke, all of which produce high quality equipment. Some amps contain the electronics and speaker(s) in one unit; others have a separate head and speaker cabinet. One of the most important things to remember when buying an amplifier is what type of music you'll be playing. For example, if you're a beginning player, you may want to start with a small practice amp that you can use at home. Even if you need to get a larger

BUYING A BASS GUITAR (continued)

amp later, you'll still be able to use your practice amp around the house. Practice amps generally cost between $100 and $250.

Bassists in a small band will probably prefer a midsize amp in the 50–100 watt range with the electronics and speakers in the same unit. A midsize amp is also a lot easier to transport. These types of amps cost from $300 to $1,000 depending on the manufacturer.

For playing large venues or outside shows, you may need a large amp. A 300 watt head with a large speaker cabinet should do nicely. When purchasing a large amp you have to take into account how you're going to move it. Be sure you have a vehicle big enough to haul this cabinet. Big amps cost between $1,200 and $2,000 and some prices go even higher. Low register frequencies resonate at a longer wave length with more vibration than higher registers, and may damage smaller speakers. Note: Don't play your bass through a friend's guitar amp—you may blow the speakers.

Always use your bass to test an amp. You may find that your particular bass doesn't sound good with certain amps. Again, don't buy an amp just for looks or name, be sure it sounds great with your bass. Also, listen critically for any buzzes or hums, because they might mean that the amp requires repairs—possibly a speaker is blown. Many amps sound completely different from a distance than they do from up close. Stand back from the amp at least 10–15 feet. You want to be sure you get a clean sound from the distance of your audience. When properly maintained, a good amp will last many years, so be sure you can live with the one you pick.

Strings

There are three basic types of strings:

Roundwound — A round wire is wrapped around a center core wire. Roundwound strings produce a sharp, bright sound and are probably the most popular strings with rock and pop bass players.

Flatwound — A flat, ribbon-like wire is wrapped around a center core.

Flatwound strings are similar to the strings on an acoustic bass, and produce a more muted, softer sound. Flatwound strings are very popular with jazz players.

Halfround — These are halfway between a roundwound and a flatwound string. Halfround strings are great if you're playing a wide variety of music.

Some well known bass string brands are Rotosound, D'Addario, Dean Markley, and Ernie Ball. Whichever type or brand of strings you choose, be aware of the gauge (thickness). Many bass manufacturers recommend a certain gauge of strings for their product. It's a good idea to follow these specs. Varying the gauge or the wind of your strings can completely change the feel or action of your instrument. If you're unhappy with the type of strings that came with your bass, find the brand you like and have the bass set up with those strings by a repair man. Also, keep a spare set of strings around in case you break one.

TUNING YOUR BASS GUITAR Track 1

Winding the Strings

If your bass came with the strings already on it (and it should have) then you won't have to worry about winding them until you're ready to change to a new set. How often you change your strings depends on how much you play. It's not a good idea to leave a set of strings on for months at a time.

When removing the strings, always change them one at a time to prevent uneven tension on the neck. After removing the old strings, don't throw them away, keep them around

as spares. Bass strings are expensive (about $20 to $30 a set), so don't waste them.

To put on a new set, start by unwrapping the new strings very carefully, without putting any kinks or bends in them. Thread the string through the appropriate hole in the back of the bridge. Pull the string all the way through until the stopper at the end of the string is resting against the bridge. The strings are secured to the tuning pegs by putting the end of the string into the hole in the center of the

string post and wrapping the rest of the slack around the post, from the top down. When the string is wound tightly around the post it should sit close to the surface of the head, firmly seated on the slot in the nut. It may be necessary to trim off the ends of some strings to get them to fit properly. Wind the string snugly around its post, but not all the way. Repeat the whole procedure with the rest of the strings. After all four strings are securely fastened, it's time to tune your bass.

TUNING YOUR BASS GUITAR (continued)

Tuning Your Bass

To get your bass in tune, you must obtain an in-tune note from an outside source. In this section we discuss the use of a tuning fork, electronic tuner and piano or other instrument.

Tuning Fork

Most tuning forks give the pitch A=440. This means they produce the note A which vibrates at 440 cycles per second. Never strike the fork against wood or metal, use your knee or elbow. After striking the fork, place the end of it against the body of your bass to hear the note A. Pluck your A string, and turn the tuning peg to tighten or loosen the string. Tune the A string to the pitch of the fork (actually the A string will be 3 octaves below the fork). This is not always easy for beginners to do, so don't get discouraged. If possible, have a musician friend help the first few times until you get the knack. Note: Remember to tighten the D string loosely (second string from the bottom) while tuning the A string to keep the tension even.

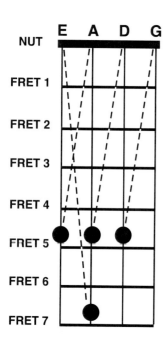

Tune the D string next. First, place the index finger of your left hand (if you're right handed) at, but not on, the 5th fret of the A string you have just tuned. Press the string to the fingerboard and pluck it with your right hand to produce the note D. Leave your finger at the 5th fret and reach across your body with your right hand and turn the D string tuning peg until the D string matches the pitch of the note on the A string. (You may have to pluck the A string a few times before you get the D string in tune.) Next, place your finger at the 5th fret of the D string. This will produce the note G. Repeat the procedure on the G string until it is in tune (remembering to tighten the E string at the same time). Lastly, place your finger at the 7th fret of the A string. This will give you the note E an octave higher than the open E string. Turn the E string tuning peg until the E string is in tune. Your bass is now in tune.

Note: When using brand new strings stretch them by flexing them between your thumb and fingers. Readjust the tuning after each stretch until they stay in tune.

Tuning with a Piano or Other Instrument

If you have access to a piano, or are in a band with a keyboard player, you will be able to tune to their instrument. The diagram below represents the piano with the keys marked which are appropriate for tuning your bass. First, find middle C—the note C closest to the middle of the keyboard. Then, play each of

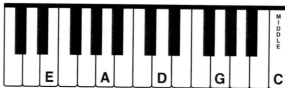

the corresponding notes and tune your strings to them. (Remember that the bass guitar actually sounds one octave below these pitches.)

When tuning with another instrument like a guitar, it's best to have someone play the notes on that instrument for you in order to be in tune with the other musicians. With a guitar, the bottom four strings are tuned exactly one octave higher than the four strings of the bass. Have the guitarist play an A and tune your A string to that pitch. Then, tune the rest of the strings with the standard method. Or, you can have the guitar player play all four notes, E, A, D, G and tune each string individually.

If you need to tune to another instrument such as a horn (trumpet, sax, etc.) just have the the horn player sound an A and do the rest yourself. You will find that the pitch A is the standard note for all instruments to tune to.

Electronic Tuners

The most common type of tuner is the digital tuner or a tuning app. Simply plug your bass into the tuner the way you would into an amplifier, or if it has a built in microphone, just play the note without a cable. Set the tuner to the appropriate note, for example, G. Some tuners will automatically tune to whatever note you are playing. Play the open G string. A read-out on a metered scale tells you if your instrument is flat (too low) or sharp (too high). Turn the tuning peg until the read-out stays in the middle of the scale. Using a digital tuner is by far the easiest way to tune your bass, but you should learn all the methods so your ear gets trained to hear when you're in tune.

GETTING STARTED

HOLDING THE BASS GUITAR

▲ *Standing*

▲ *Sitting, with bass on right leg*

FINGER STYLE OR PICK STYLE?

Ideally you should be able to play either way. Playing with the fingers will probably give you more speed and flexibility, but many rock players prefer the pick because of its harder sound and sharper attack. Read the descriptions of both styles below, try them, then make your own decision. The music in this book can be played either way.

Playing the Bass Guitar Finger Style

Many of the stars on the instrument use alternate strokes of the index and middle fingers of the right hand to produce the notes. The photos show you how to do this. Especially see that after striking the string, the finger comes to rest on the next string.

To get the feel of this, play a series of notes on the open 1st string. Keep a steady beat and use alternate strokes of the index and middle finger.

Index finger

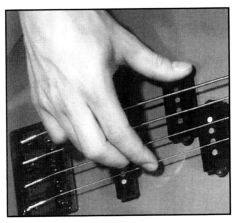

▲ *In position*

▲ *After striking the 1st string*

Middle finger

▲ *In position*

▲ *After striking the 1st string*

FINGER STYLE OR PICK STYLE? (continued)

Playing the Bass Guitar Pick Style

Many players, especially rock musicians, prefer to use a pick. The pick is a triangular shaped piece of flat plastic which is held between the thumb and 1st finger of the right hand.

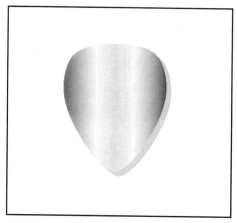

▲ *The pick*

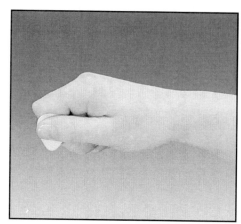

▲ *Holding the pick*

Action of the Pick

To get the feel of playing with a pick, play a series of notes on the open G string. Keep a steady beat and use only down-picks (toward the floor) for now.

▲ *In position*

▲ *After striking the 1st string*

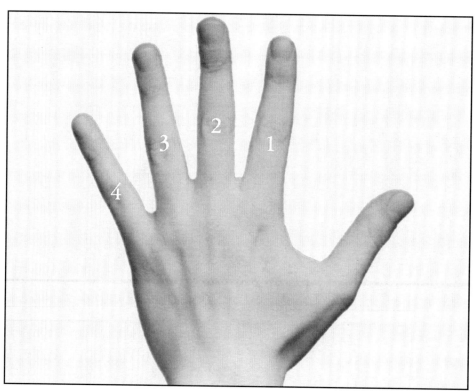

▲ *Numbering the left-hand fingers*

GETTING ACQUAINTED WITH MUSIC

Notes

Musical sounds are indicated by symbols called NOTES. Their time value is determined by their color (white or black) and by stems and flags attached to the note.

The Staff

The name and pitch of the notes are determined by the note's position on a graph made of five horizontal lines and the spaces in between, called the staff. The notes are named after the first seven letters of the alphabet (A–G), repeated to embrace the entire range of musical sound.

You may want to use this simple memorization trick to remember the notes:

On the lines:
Good **B**oys **D**o **F**ine **A**lways
In the spaces: **A**ll **C**ows **E**at **G**rass

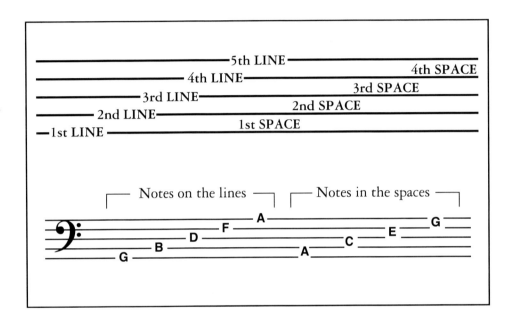

Measures and Bar Lines

Music is also divided into equal parts, called MEASURES. One measure is divided from another by a BAR LINE.

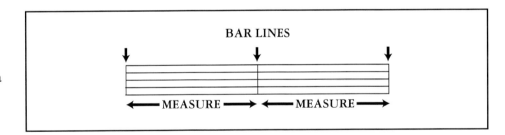

Clefs

Music for the bass guitar is written in the bass clef. The symbol for the bass clef is derived from the Old German way of writing the letter F:

(some books refer to the bass clef as the F clef). The two dots straddle the 4th line of the staff, and this line is indeed the note F.

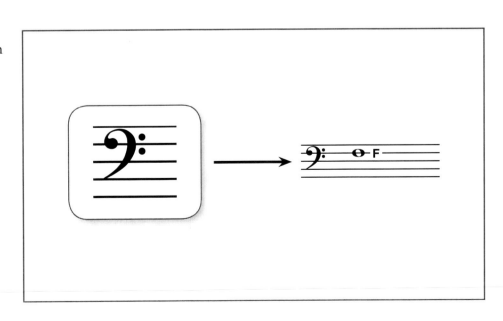

GETTING ACQUAINTED WITH TABLATURE

All the music in this book is written two ways. Below each traditional music staff you'll find a four line tablature staff. Each line represents a string of the bass guitar, with the highest or thinnest string at the top and the lowest or thickest string at the bottom.

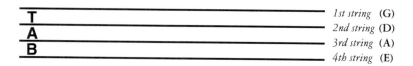

The numbers placed on the tablature lines tell you which fret to play. A zero means to play the string open (not fingered).

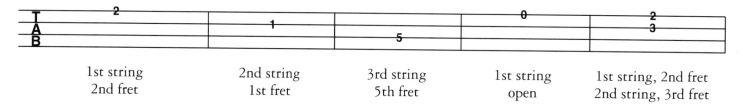

1st string	2nd string	3rd string	1st string	1st string, 2nd fret
2nd fret	1st fret	5th fret	open	2nd string, 3rd fret

By glancing at the tablature staff you can immediately tell where to play a note. Although you can't tell exactly what the rhythm is from the tablature, the horizontal spacing of the numbers gives you a strong hint about how fast or slow the notes are to be played.

SOUND OFF: HOW TO COUNT TIME

4 Kinds of Notes:

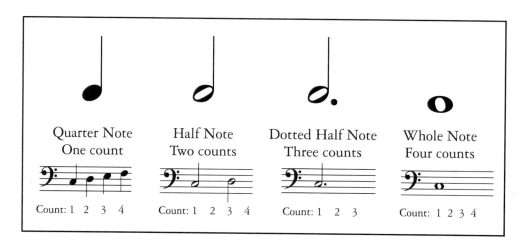

Time Signatures

Each piece of music has two numbers at its beginning called a time signature. These numbers tell us how to count time for that particular piece.

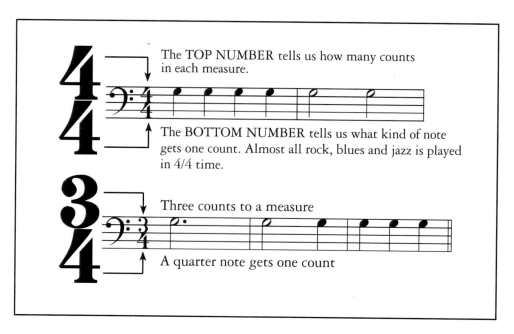

Notes on the G or 1st String

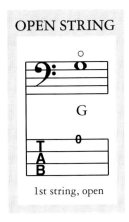

1st string, open

The basic rhythm of every type of music from classical to heavy metal is the *quarter note*. To play quarter notes, tap a steady beat with your foot. Then play one note for each foot tap or count. (Play these exercises on the 1st string— open G string.)

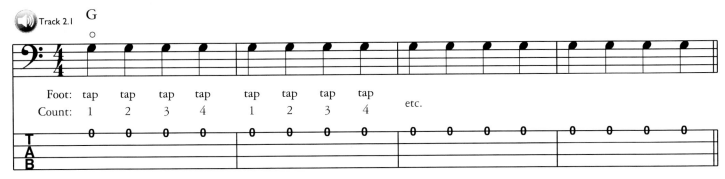

Half notes are held twice as long as quarter notes, that is, for two foot taps or beats.

Dotted half notes are held for three foot taps or beats.

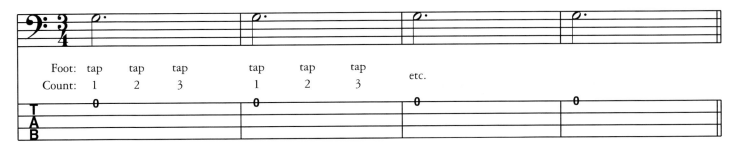

Whole notes are held for four foot taps or beats.

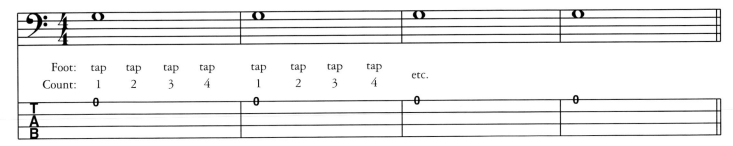

Notes on the G or 1st String

2nd FRET

1st string, 2nd fret

Placing the 2nd finger on the 2nd fret of the G string produces the note A.

Play the following exercises which combine the fingered note A with the rhythms you have learned.

Quarter Note	Half Note	Dotted Half Note	Whole Note
1 Beat	2 Beats	3 Beats	4 Beats

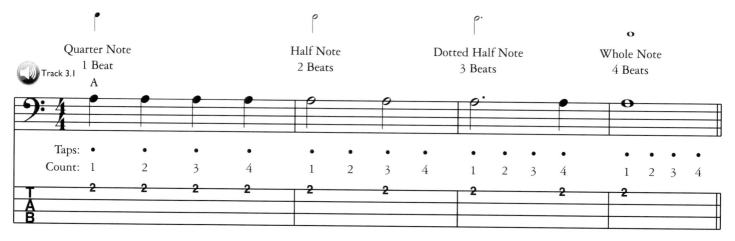

Track 3.1

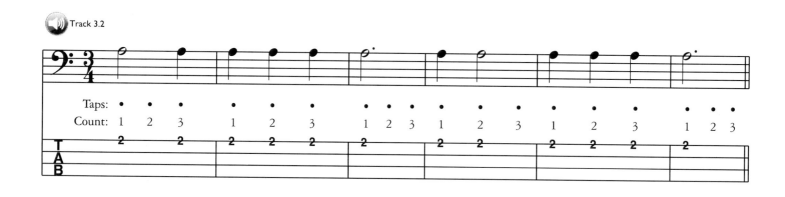

Track 3.2

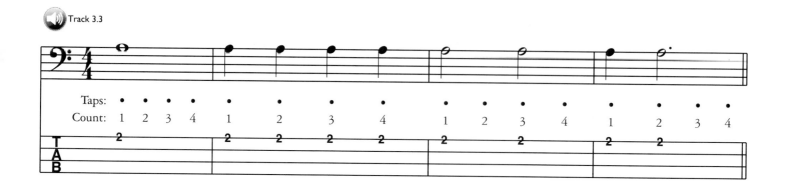

Track 3.3

Practice the following exercises which combine the open G string, the fingered note A and all the rhythms you have learned. When playing the A, make sure you press down hard, close to the fret.

Track 4.1

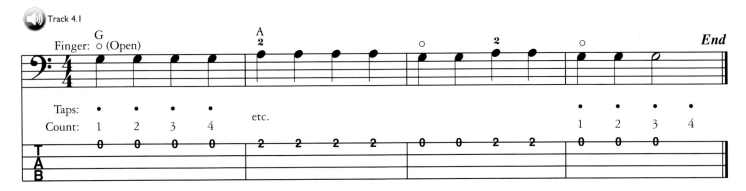

Track 4.2

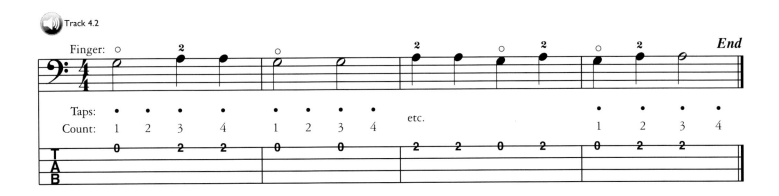

Track 4.3

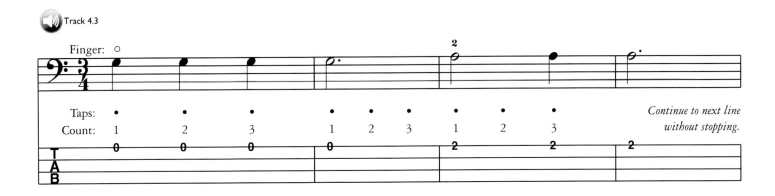

Track 4.4

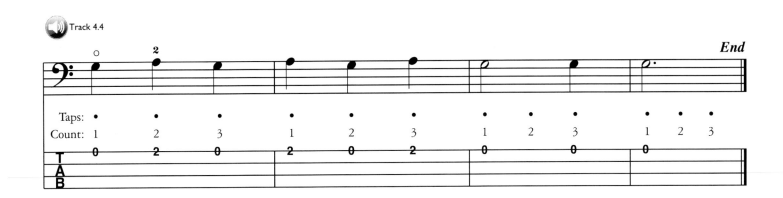

RESTS

In music, a *rest* is a measured silence. To get a clean sound, here's how to play rests on the bass guitar.

If the note is open (like the G you've just learned), stop the vibration of the string with the fingers of the left hand. If the note is fingered (like the A) release the pressure on the string but keep the finger touching it.

▲ *Stop the vibrations of an open note with your fingers.*

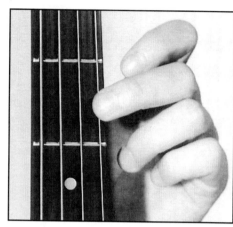

▲ *Stop the vibrations of a fingered note by releasing pressure on the string.*

The three basic rests are:

QUARTER REST	HALF REST	WHOLE REST

One beat of silence   Two beats of silence   A whole measure of silence (four beats in 4/4 time, three beats in 3/4 time)

An easy way to remember the difference between the half and whole rest is to think of the whole rest as being longer (or heavier) and so hangs below the line. The half rest is shorter (or lighter) and so sits on top of the line.

Practice the following exercises which combine rests with the notes and rhythms you have already learned.

Track 5.1

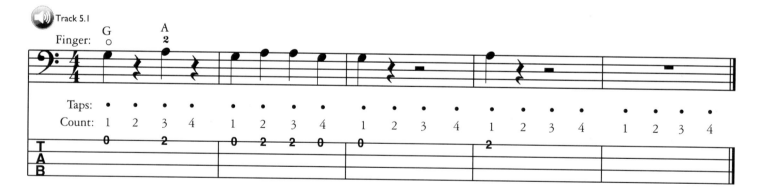

Track 5.2

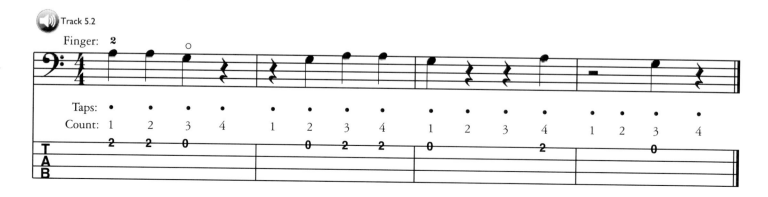

Notes on the D or Second String

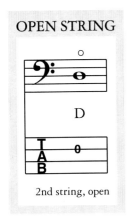

OPEN STRING

D

2nd string, open

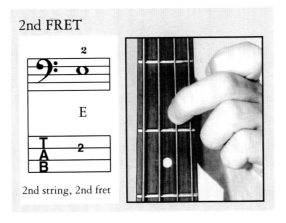

2nd FRET

E

2nd string, 2nd fret

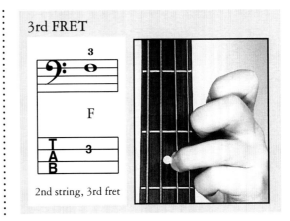

3rd FRET

F

2nd string, 3rd fret

If you have difficulty making a clear sound when playing the note F using the 3rd finger, try adding the 4th finger until you build up the strength of your third finger.

▲ *WRONG*
Finger is too far from fret;
sound is "buzzy" and unclear.

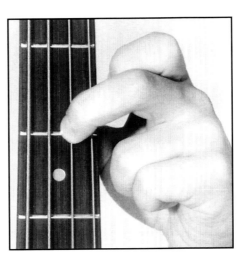

▲ *WRONG*
Finger is on top of the fret;
sound is muffled and unclear.

▲ *RIGHT*
Finger is close to the fret
without actually touching it.

Track 6

PLAYING NOTES (D-E-F) ON THE D STRING

Track 7.1

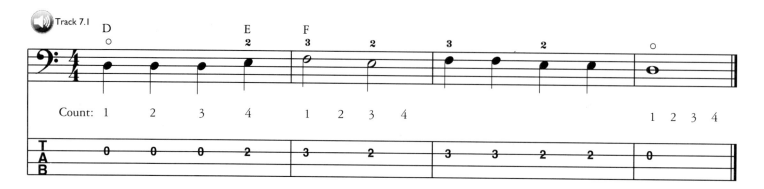

Track 7.2

Continue to next line without stopping.

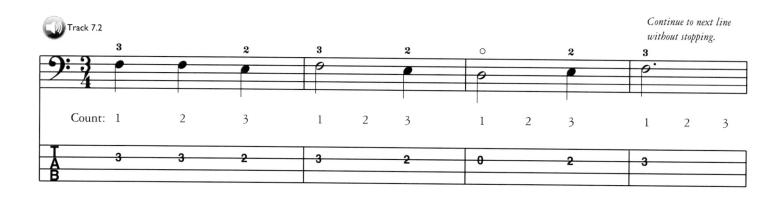

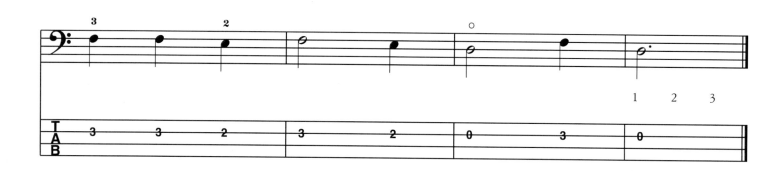

Track 7.3

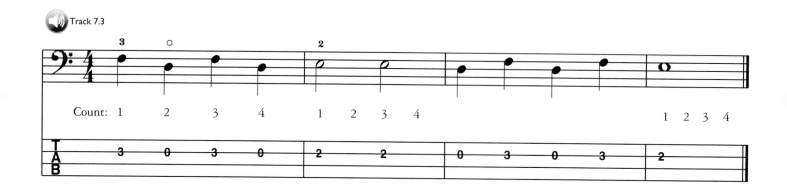

PLAYING NOTES ON THE G (G-A) AND D (D-E-F) STRINGS

Use this first exercise as part of a daily warm-up.
Play it many times, keeping a steady beat and go for a clean, clear sound.

Many early rock tunes were based on the blues. The following bass line can be used for a D minor blues. The chord symbols are for keyboard or guitar, in case you have a friend you can play with.

Minor Blues Rock
Track 8.2

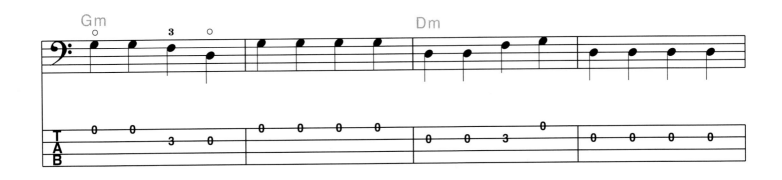

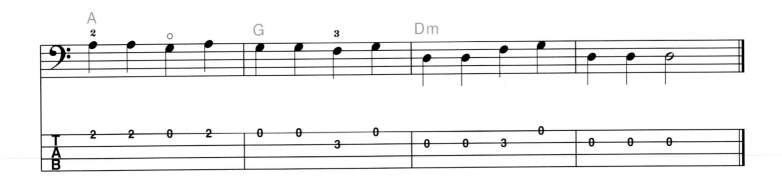

Notes on the A or 3rd String

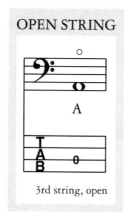

OPEN STRING

A

3rd string, open

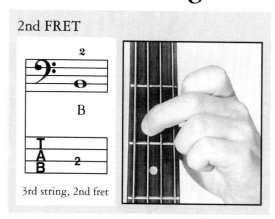

2nd FRET

B

3rd string, 2nd fret

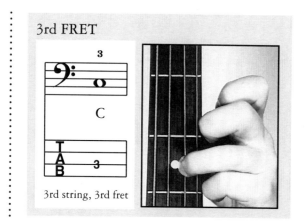

3rd FRET

C

3rd string, 3rd fret

UP STEMS AND DOWN STEMS

Until now, all notes have been written with the stems down ⌐. To make the music look neater, down *and* up stems are used.

Notes ABOVE or ON the middle line have stems pointing DOWN.

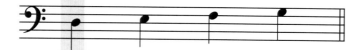

Notes BELOW the middle line have stems pointing UP.

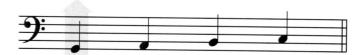

Track 9.1

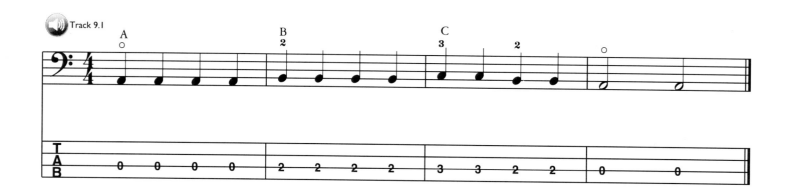

Track 9.2

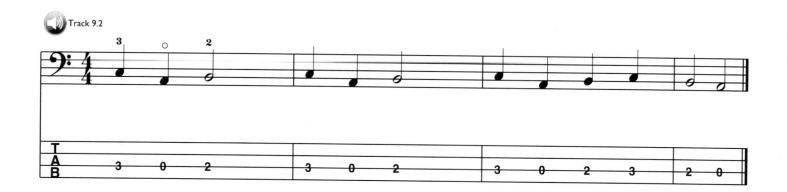

THE NATURAL MINOR SCALE

A scale is a set of seven notes with a specific arrangement of whole and half steps. Each scale has a different sound because of its unique arrangement of these intervals.

The natural minor scale in A is also known as the Aeolian mode. This scale includes every note you've learned so far. Play it many times as part of a daily warm-up. Keep the beat steady and get a clean sound!

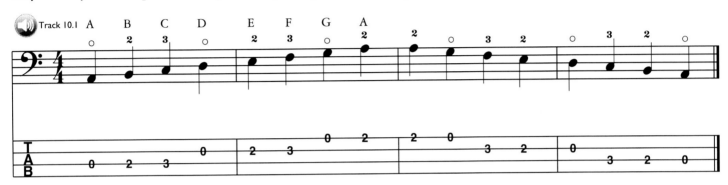

Rockin' à la Mode

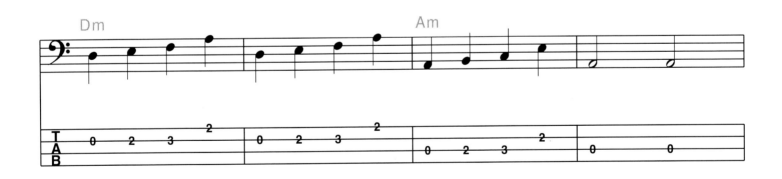

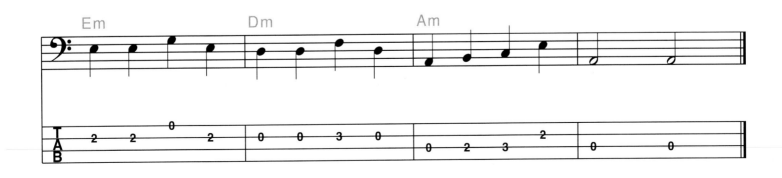

SHARPS ♯♯

A sharp placed before a note means to play that note one fret higher than usual. If the note is usually played on the *open* string, finger the sharped note on the 1st fret with the 1st finger.

If the note is usually *fingered*, play the sharped note one fret higher.

Since the note E♯ is the same as F, it is not used much. The same goes for B♯ which is the same as C.

A sharp stays in effect for a whole measure: Track 11.1

The bar line restores a sharped note to its usual position. Track 11.2

A natural sign ♮ cancels a previous sharp sign within the measure. Track 11.3 A natural sign may be used in a new measure to remind you that a note is no longer sharped.

Notes on the Fourth Fret

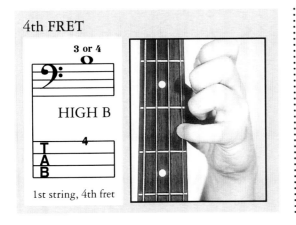

4th FRET

3 or 4

HIGH B

1st string, 4th fret

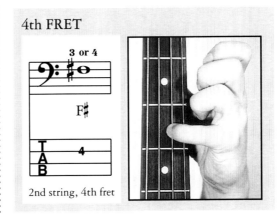

4th FRET

3 or 4

F♯

2nd string, 4th fret

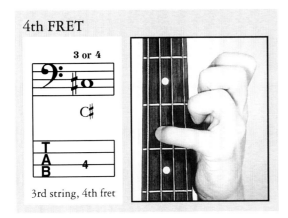

4th FRET

3 or 4

C♯

3rd string, 4th fret

You can play notes on the 4th fret with either your 4th finger or, if you do not have enough finger strength at this time, you can shift your 3rd finger up to the 4th fret.

Practice these exercises which include notes on the 4th fret and other sharped notes.

Track 12.1

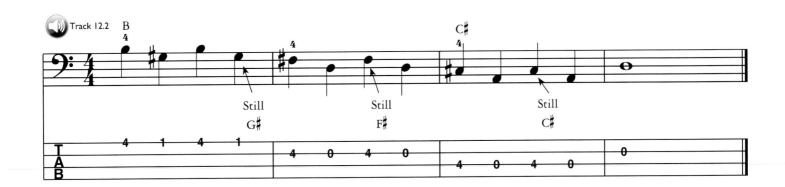

Track 12.2

Notes on the E or Fourth String

OPEN STRING

Leger Line* E

4th string, open

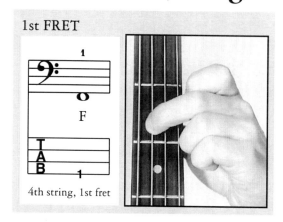

1st FRET

F

4th string, 1st fret

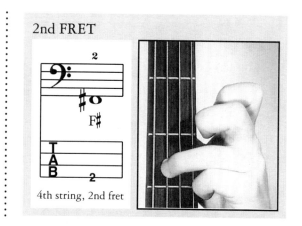

2nd FRET

F♯

4th string, 2nd fret

ATTENTION FINGER STYLE PLAYERS!

When playing on the E string, the fingers of the right hand come to rest against the pick guard.

3rd FRET

G

4th string, 3rd fret

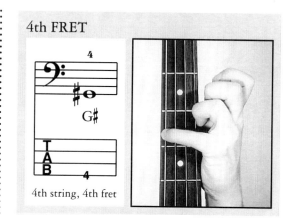

4th FRET

G♯

4th string, 4th fret

The E string, being the largest, is the most difficult string to play. Make sure you're pressing very hard with the left hand, close to the fret without being on it! Track 13

*LEGER LINES The short line that extends the staff downward is called a *leger* line. On bass guitar, only the low E requires a leger line below the staff.

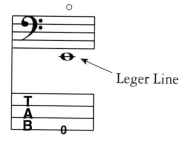

Leger Line

NOTE FINDING REVIEW

The following exercise uses every note and sharp you've learned so far. Practice it until you can play it without missing a beat.   Track 14.1

When you can play this review smoothly, you are well on your way to becoming a good bass player.

Bass Line for a Swing Tune   Track 14.2

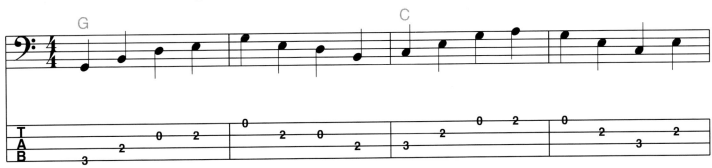

FLATS ♭

A flat placed before a note means to play that note one fret lower than usual. If the note is usually *fingered* on the 2nd fret, play the flat on the 1st fret. If it's usually played on the 3rd fret, play the flat on the 2nd fret, and so on.

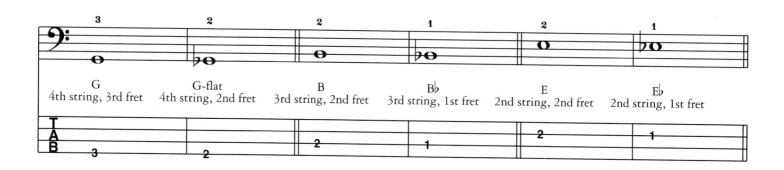

Since the note F♭ is the same as E, it's not used much. The same goes for C♭ which is the same as B.

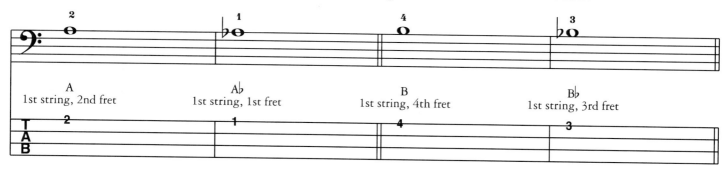

To flat a note usually played on an *open* string, play the next *lower* string on the 4th fret.

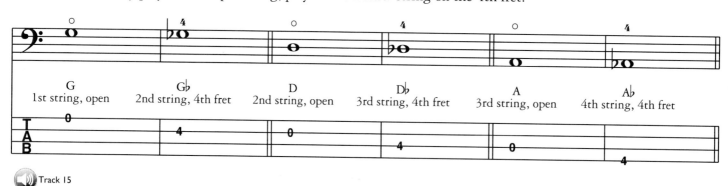

Track 15

The rules for flats are the same as sharps: a barline restores a flatted note to its usual position. A natural sign ♮ cancels a previous flat within the measure (and sometimes in the next measure as a reminder).

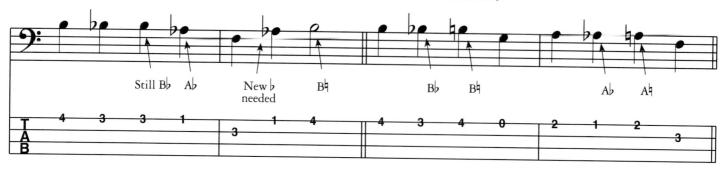

NOTE FINDING REVIEW

Practice the following exercises until you can play them without missing a beat.

Flats and Naturals Track 16.1

Flats, Sharps and Naturals Track 16.2

KEY SIGNATURES

Key Signature

The flats or sharps placed at the beginning of every line are called the *key signature*. One flat means to play every B note as a Bb, unless preceded by a natural sign. First practice the scale, then play the exercise and song.

THE MAJOR SCALE

The major scale is a series of seven notes separated by *half-steps* (next fret) and *whole-steps* (skip a fret).

The sequence is always: W W H W W W H.

The F Major Scale   Track 17.1

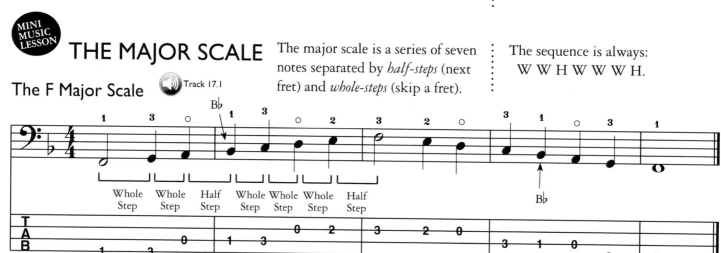

The one-flat key signature also tells you that the piece is in the key of F. The following exercise extends the F major scale to the high Bb. Notice that pieces in the key of F almost always end on the note F. A key is kind of a musical "home base" from which the music departs and eventually returns.

Rockin' in F   Track 17.3

*A repeat sign at the end of a piece means to go back to the beginning and play the entire piece again.

THE KEY OF B♭

A key signature of two flats tells you the piece is in the key of B♭. All B's are played as B♭ and all E's are played as E♭ unless preceded by a natural sign. First practice the scale, then play the exercises.

The B♭ Major Scale   Track 18.1

Moderate Jazz Blues in B♭   Track 18.2

* Notes that appear in a key that do not belong to that key (such as the E♮ and A♭ in this piece) are called *accidentals*.

EIGHTH NOTES

Eighth notes are black notes with a flag added to the stem ♪ or ♩. Two or more eighth notes are written with connecting stems, ♫ or ♫, ♫♫ or ♫♫.

Whole Note   2 Half Notes   4 Quarter Notes   8 Eighth Notes

Eighth notes on an open string   Track 19.1

Remember—Repeat Sign: go back to the ‖: and play again.

Eighth notes on three open strings   Track 19.2

Eighth notes with fingered notes   Track 19.3

The following exercises in the keys of F and B♭ combine eighth notes with other rhythms and make use of most of the notes you've learned. Serious students will want to add this page to their daily warm-ups.

In F   Track 20.1

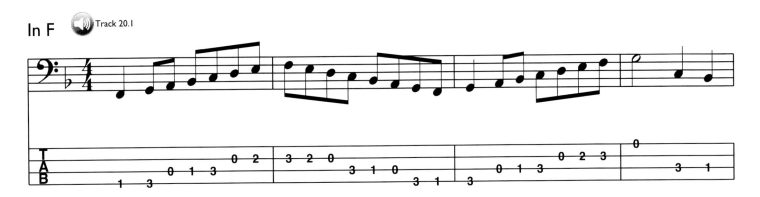

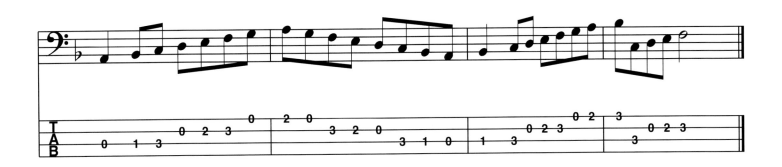

In B♭   Track 20.2

In B♭   Track 20.3

BASS LICKS IN THE KEYS OF F AND B♭

A "lick" is a short phrase, usually one or two measures, that musicians use to fill in dead spots in the music and to add interest to their playing.

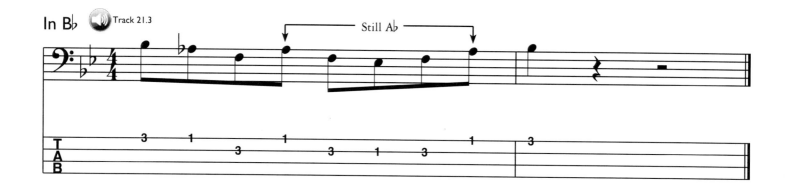

THE KEY OF G

The key signature of one sharp tells you a piece is in the key of G. All F's are played as F♯ unless preceded by a natural sign.

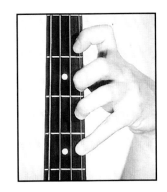

THE 2nd POSITION

The G Major scale below is played in the 2nd position. This means that the left hand is shifted up the fingerboard so that the 1st finger plays notes on the 2nd fret; the 2nd finger plays notes on the 3rd fret; the 3rd finger plays notes on the 4th fret; and the 4th finger plays notes on the 5th fret

Learn the scale and add it to your daily practice, then practice the exercises.

INTRODUCING TIES

Ties are curved lines connecting two or more successive notes of the same pitch. When two notes are tied, the second one is not picked, its time value is added to the value of the first note.

INTRODUCING DOTTED QUARTER NOTES

A DOT INCREASES THE LENGTH OF A NOTE BY ONE-HALF!

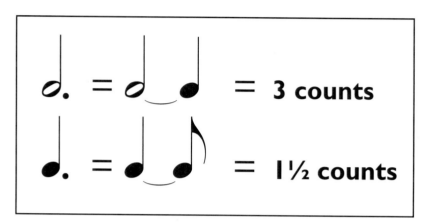

Preparatory Drill Track 23.1

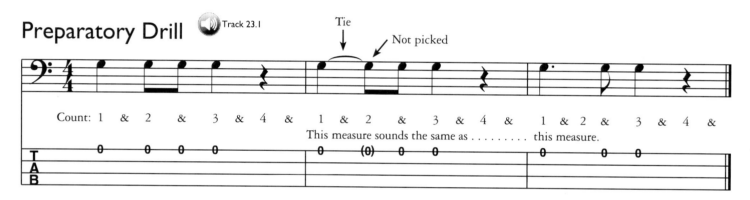

In TAB notation, the tie is indicated by a parenthesis — do not pick that note again.

Rock Bass Line in G Track 23.2

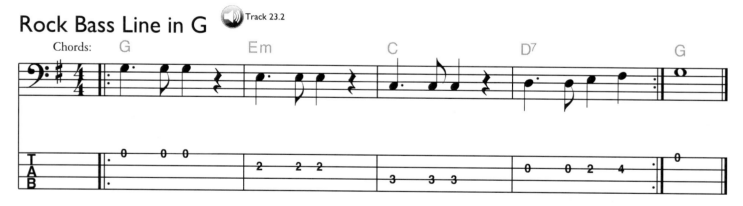

Rock Bass Line in F Track 23.3

INTRODUCING THE SLIDE

Slide

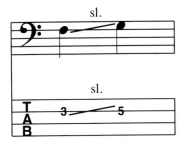

Sound the lower (first) note, then slide the fret finger up to sound the higher (second) note. The higher note is not picked again.

Slide Up

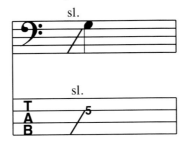

Sound the string as your fret hand slides up to the desired note.

Below are some examples of slides used in Country bass licks.

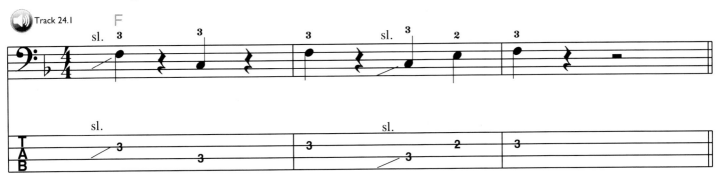

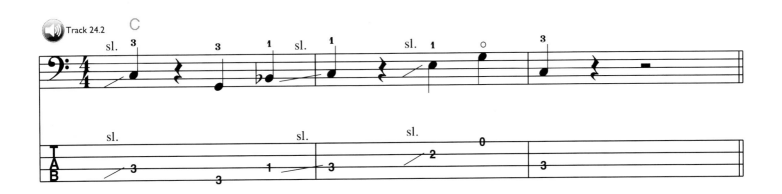

THE ACCENTED NOTE

The picking hand plays the accented notes (>) by plucking the string harder than the non-accented notes.

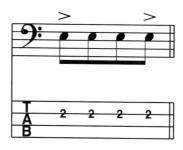

Below are examples of accented notes used in Heavy Metal bass licks.

Track 25.1

Track 25.2

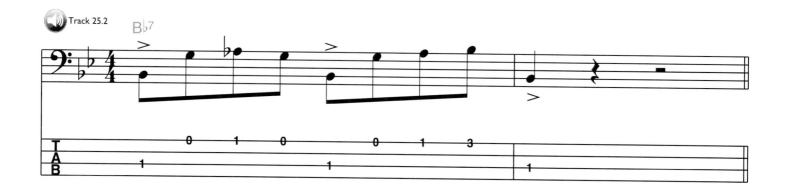

Track 25.3

LICKS AND EXERCISES WITH DOTTED QUARTER NOTES, ACCENTS AND SLIDES

Track 26.1

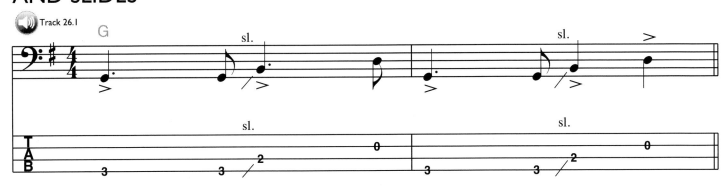

Track 26.2

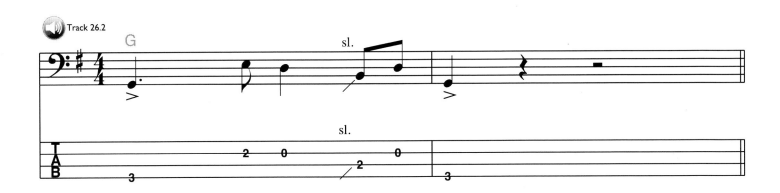

G Major Exercise   Track 26.3

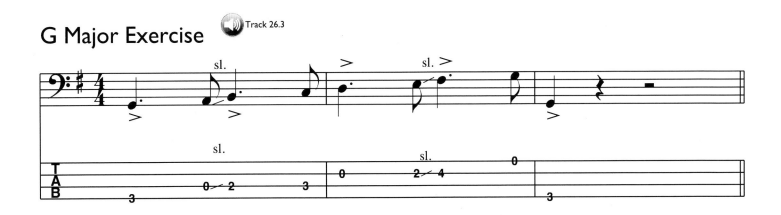

G Major Exercise   Track 26.4

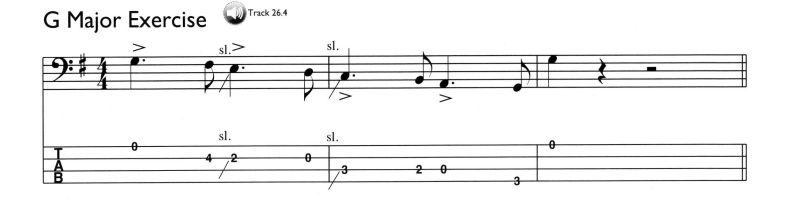

The 3rd Position

The hand in 3rd position	Playing High C	Playing G on the D String
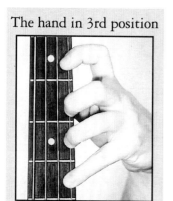	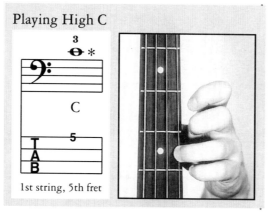	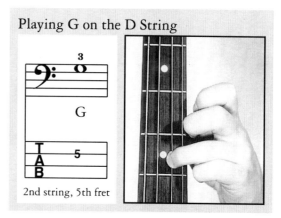

▲ *Shift the left hand so that the 1st finger plays the notes on the 3rd fret, the 2nd finger plays the notes on the 4th fret, and the 3rd finger plays the notes on the 5th fret.*

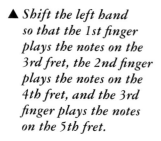

Playing D on the A String	Playing A on the E String
	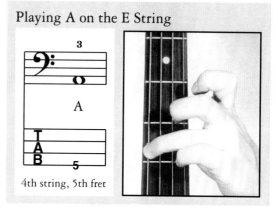

* Leger lines (p.22) also extend the staff upward. Theoretically, there is no limit to the number of leger lines. In this book we won't go past three.

Notice that you now have alternate ways of playing G, D, and A. Compare the following:

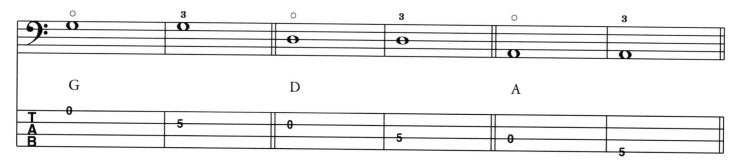

It's impossible to give a hard and fast rule about whether to use the open or fingered form of a note. Many players avoid using open strings altogether. The best policy is to try a passage both ways and pick the one that's easier to play and gets the better sound.

For example, most players would find the first fingering of the following passage easier to play.

THE KEY OF C

A key signature without sharps or flats tells you a piece is in the key of C. All notes are played natural unless preceded by a sharp or flat. First practice the scale, then play the exercises and bass line. Fingering on some notes will change depending on your hand position.

The C Major Scale  Track 27.1

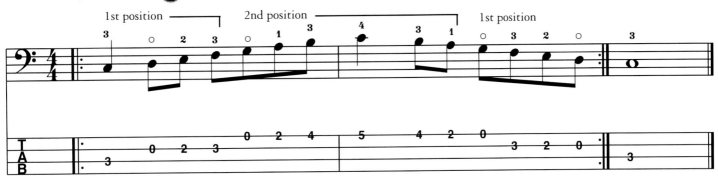

Track 27.2

Bass Line for a Rocker Track 27.3

SYNCOPATION

Syncopation is a musical effect in which a note is anticipated, that is, played before its expected beat. Syncopation is very important to all forms of popular music. Without it, jazz, rock, country, blues, heavy metal and other types of pop music could not exist as we know them.

In the examples below, first play the un-syncopated or "straight" version of the rhythm. Then play the syncopated version. For best results, count carefully and accent (play louder) all anticipated notes.

Example 1 is not syncopated—Each

quarter note falls in the expected place, on the beat. Example 2 is a simple syncopation. The 3rd quarter note is played early, on the "and" of the 2nd beat rather than in its expected place on the 3rd beat.

 Track 28.1

 Track 28.2

Ex. 1   Un-syncopated or "straight" version of the rhythm.   Ex. 2   3rd beat anticipated.

 Track 28.3

 Track 28.4

Ex. 3   Whole note anticipated across the bar line.   Ex. 4   2nd beat anticipated.

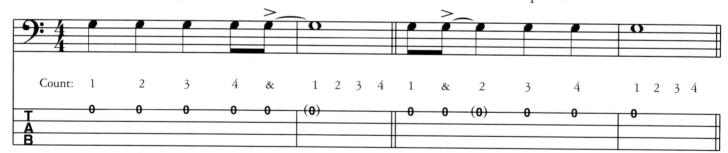

 Track 28.5

 Track 28.6

Ex. 5   2nd and 3rd beats anticipated.   Ex. 6   2nd, 3rd and 4th beats anticipated.

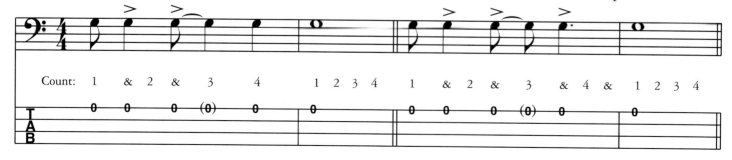

SYNCOPATED EXERCISES IN VARIOUS KEYS

Remember to count carefully and to accent all anticipated notes.

Key of C Track 29.1

Key of G Track 29.2

Key of F Track 29.3

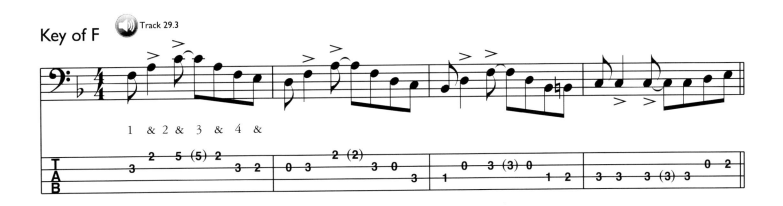

Key of B♭ Track 29.4

ROCK BASS LICKS WITH SYNCOPATION

Track 30.1

Track 30.2

Track 30.3

Track 30.4

HEAVY METAL BASS LICKS WITH SYNCOPATION

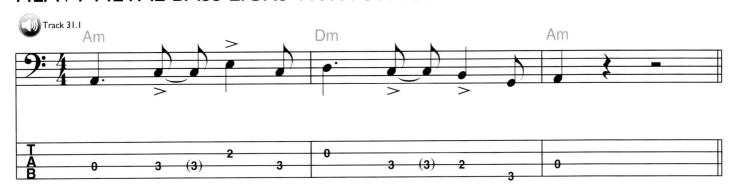

Track 31.1

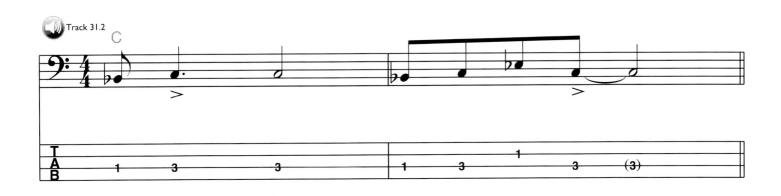

Track 31.2

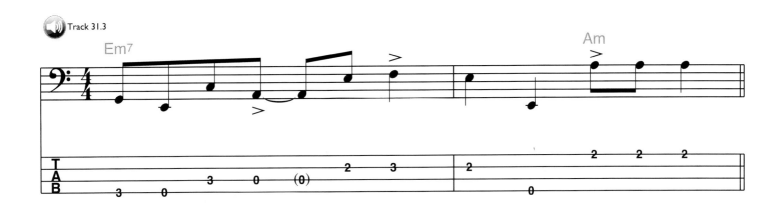

Track 31.3

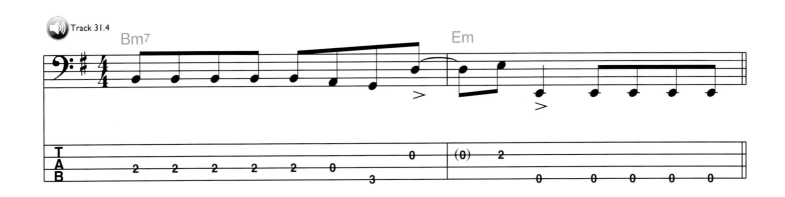

Track 31.4

Notes Above High C, Part 1

To extend the upper range of the notes you've learned so far, play the following:

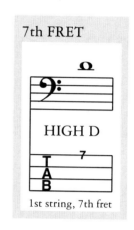

Fingering on some notes will vary depending on context (what precedes and what follows).

Exercise with High C♯ and D

Exercise with High D♭

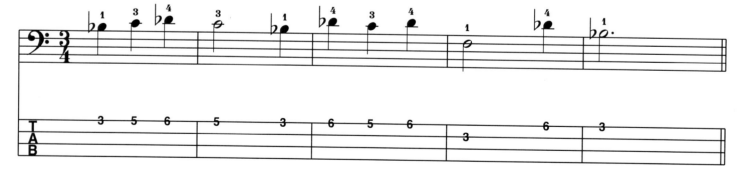

THE KEY OF D

A key signature of two sharps tells you a piece is in the key of D. All F's are played as F♯ and all C's are played as C♯ unless preceded by a natural sign.

Your new knowledge of the high C♯ and D notes allows you to play a D major scale up to the high D. Practice it, then play the other material on the page.

The D Major Scale — Track 33.1

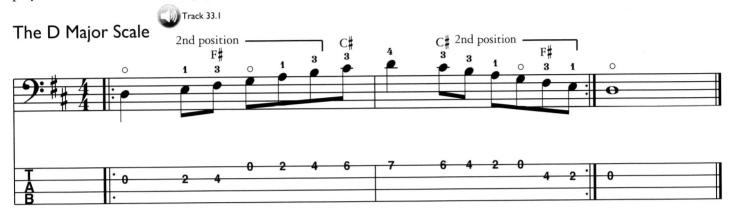

Fragment from "Joy to the World" — Track 33.2

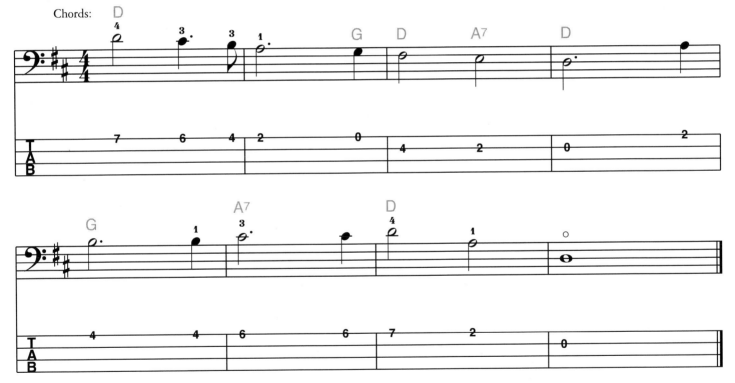

The D Scale with Repeated Notes — Track 33.3

Rock Licks in G, C and D

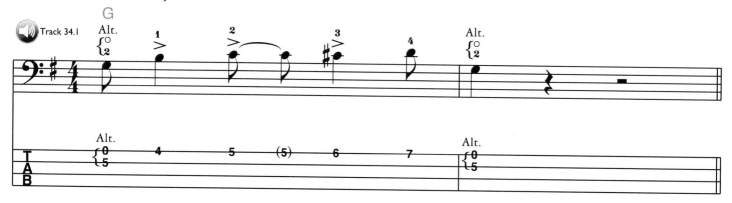

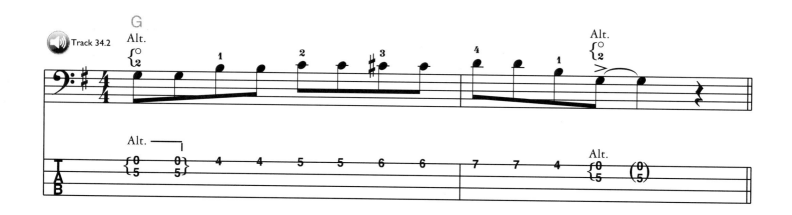

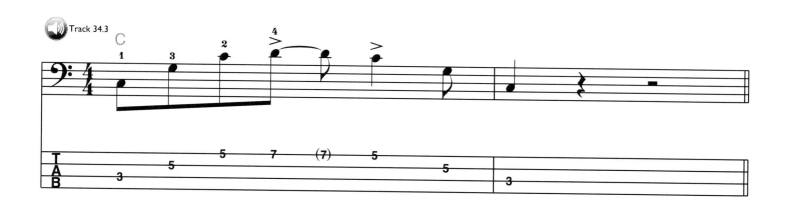

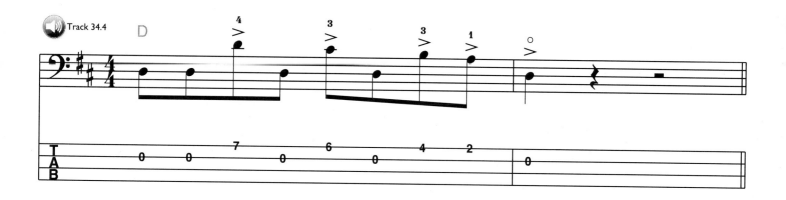

Heavy Metal Licks in G, C and D

Track 35.1

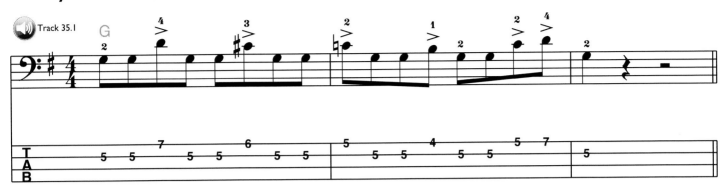

When moving up or down the neck and changing strings, it is sometimes easier if you use the 4th finger to play notes you would usually play with the 3rd.

Track 35.2

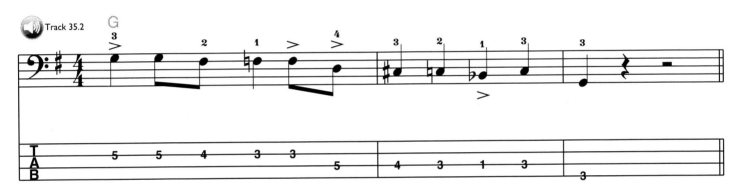

Track 35.3

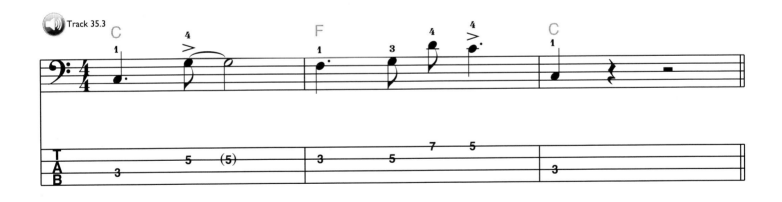

Track 35.4

THE DOTTED 8th and 16th NOTE RHYTHM

Like 8th notes, dotted 8ths and 16ths are played two to each beat. But unlike 8th notes (which are played evenly) dotted 8ths and 16ths are played unevenly: long, short, long, short.

Compare the following:

An easy way to remember the sound of dotted 8ths and 16ths is to say the words:

The dotted 8th and 16th note rhythm is very common in tunes played with a "shuffle beat" such as "Kansas City," "Rock Around the Clock" and many other early blues-based rock tunes. Practice the two exercises below, then play the licks on page 47.

Track 36.1

Track 36.2

Blues in C

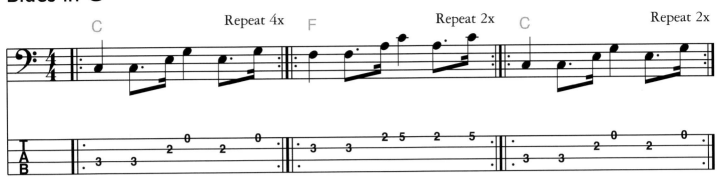

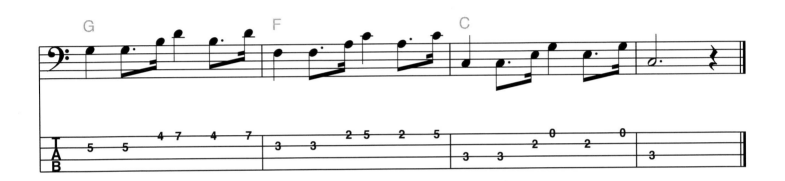

In D

In F

THE KEY OF A

A key signature of three sharps tells you the piece is in the key of A. All F's are played as F♯, all C's are played as C♯, and all G's are played as G♯, unless preceded by a natural sign.

Because it is an especially good sounding key on guitar, the key of A is very popular in rock and country groups.

Practice the A major scale below, then play the other material on the page.

The A Major Scale   Track 38.1

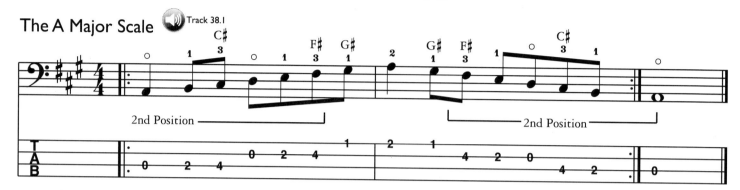

 ## Incomplete Measures

Music sometimes begins with an incomplete measure, called the *up-beat* or *pick-up*. If the up-beat is one beat, the last measure will often have only three beats in $\frac{4}{4}$, or two beats in $\frac{3}{4}$. If the up-beats are three beats, the last measure will often have only one beat in $\frac{4}{4}$.

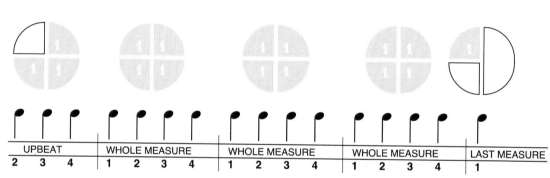

Bass Line for a Country Song   Track 38.2

*D.C. stands for the Italian *da capo*, literally "from the head." It means to repeat the entire piece from the beginning. Notice that the piece begins on the 2nd beat of the measure. Since the last measure has only one beat, it and the three beats in the 1st measure combine to make one complete measure of $\frac{4}{4}$ time.

BASS LICKS IN A

Track 39.1

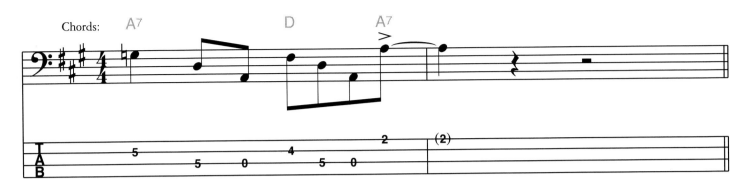

Track 39.2

Track 39.3

Track 39.4

INTRODUCING TRIPLETS

A triplet is a group of three notes played in the time of two. For example, two 8th notes are played in one beat. Three 8th notes with a "3" over or under them are called an 8th note triplet; they are played faster than 8th notes so that the three notes are played in the time of two regular 8th notes. You can remember the sound of 8th note triplets by saying the words "mer-ri-ly, mer-ri-ly." Each word sounds like an 8th note triplet.

The exercises below contrast 8th note triplets with other rhythms.

Track 40.1

In the early days of rock, a type of ballad developed that depended on the triplet rhythm. Called "doo-wop," they are played slowly with a steady flow of triplets, as in this example.

Track 40.2

Slowly

BASS LICKS WITH TRIPLETS

Track 41.1

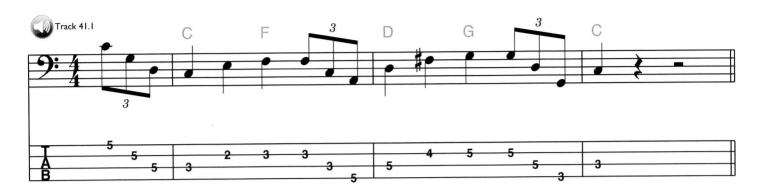

Track 41.2

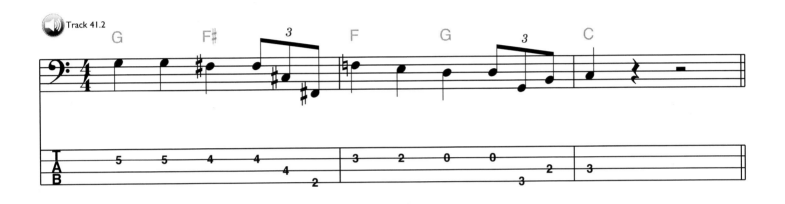

Track 41.3

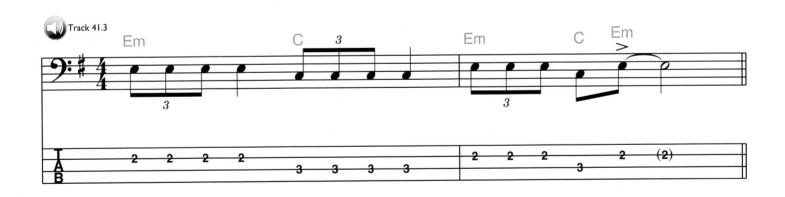

Track 41.4

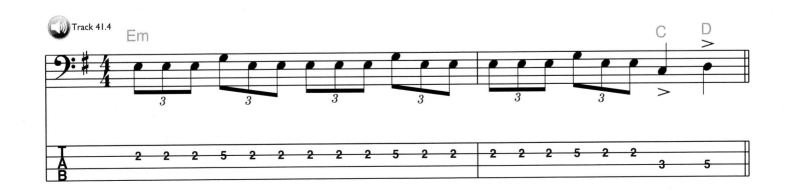

THE KEY OF E MAJOR

A key signature of four sharps tells you a piece is in the key of E. All F's are played as F#, C's are played as C#, G's are played as G#, D's are played as D# unless preceded by a natural sign.

As with the key of A, the key of E is very important in rock, blues and country music because it sounds good on the guitar.

Practice the scale, then the exercises.

The E Major Scale Track 42.1

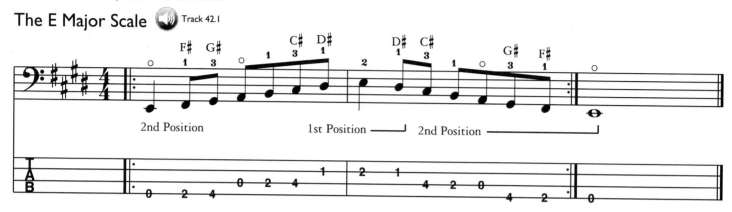

Track 42.2

Track 42.3

Notes Above High C, Part 2

To extend your upper register even further, play the following:

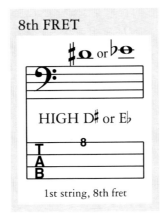

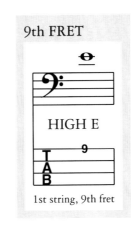

As with the notes learned on page 42, fingering will depend on what precedes and what follows the note you're playing.

Exercise with High D♯ and E.   Track 43.1

Exercise with High E♭   Track 43.2

Your knowledge of the high D♯ and E notes allows you to play an E major scale in two octaves. Add the following to your daily practice.

The Two-Octave E Major Scale.   Track 43.3

BASS LICKS IN E MAJOR

Track 44.1

Track 44.2

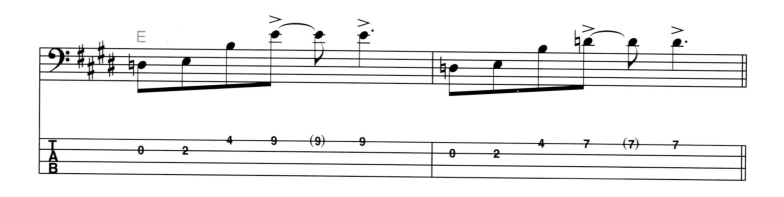

Track 44.3

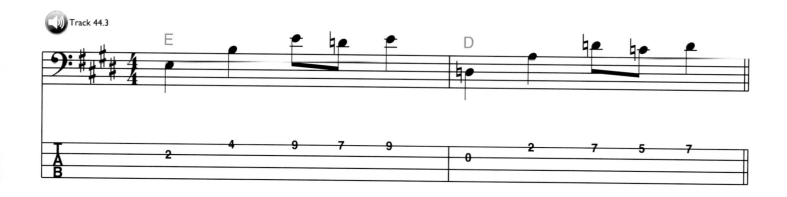

INTRODUCING CHORDS

Often the bass guitar is expected to play from a chord sheet, like the ones guitar players use. You, as a bass guitarist, are expected to come up with an effective bass line based on the chords.

What Is a Chord?

A chord is a group of three or more notes that sound good when played together.

What Kinds of Chords Are There?

In rock, blues, country and other popular styles, most of the chords used fall into three types: major chords, minor chords, and seventh chords.

The symbol for a major chord is a capital letter such as C, G, F♯, or E♭. That is, if you see E♭ on a chord sheet, it means "E♭ major chord."

The symbol for a minor chord is a small m as in Cm, F♯m, or E♭m. If you see Cm on a chord sheet, it means "C minor chord."

The symbol for a seventh chord is a capital letter followed by the number 7 as in G7, D7, F♯7, or A♭7. By the way, say: G seventh, not G seven.

What Notes Do Chords Contain?

The most important note of a chord is called the *root*. This is the note that names the chord; for example, the root of a C major chord is the note C. The root of a D minor chord is the note D. The root of an F♯7 chord is the note F♯, and so on. Other notes are called the 3rd, 5th and (in 7th chords) the 7th.

The chart below gives you the notes contained in every common major, minor and 7th chord. (For a more complete chart see page 79.)

Serious students will want to memorize this chart, as the information in it will be used over and over again.

Major Chords

		Root	3rd	5th
A	=	A	C♯	E
B♭	=	B♭	D	F
B	=	B	D♯	F♯
C	=	C	E	G
D	=	D	F♯	A
E♭	=	E♭	G	B♭
E	=	E	G♯	B
F	=	F	A	C
G	=	G	B	D

Minor Chords

		Root	3rd	5th
Am	=	A	C	E
B♭m	=	B♭	D♭	F
Bm	=	B	D	F♯
Cm	=	C	E♭	G
Dm	=	D	F	A
E♭m	=	E♭	G♭	B♭
Em	=	E	G	B
Fm	=	F	A♭	C
Gm	=	G	B♭	D

Seventh Chords

		Root	3rd	5th	7th
A7	=	A	C♯	E	G
B♭7	=	B♭	D	F	A♭
B7	=	B	D♯	F♯	A
C7	=	C	E	G	B♭
D7	=	D	F♯	A	C
E♭7	=	E♭	G	B♭	D♭
E7	=	E	G♯	B	D
F7	=	F	A	C	E♭
Gm	=	G	B♭	D	F

PLAYING FROM CHORD SHEETS, Part I

Here's a typical rock progression from the early rock days:

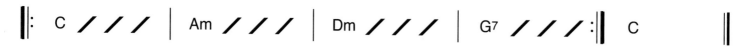

Track 45.1 The simplest thing you can do is play each root as a whole note. Even this simple device can be effective on the right song, say a doo-wop ballad like the Platters' 1955 hit, "Only You."

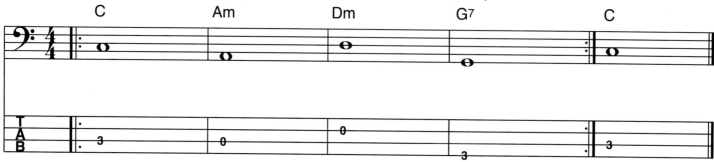

Track 45.2 On a bright rhythm tune like "Why Must I Be A Teenager in Love?" half notes can be very effective.

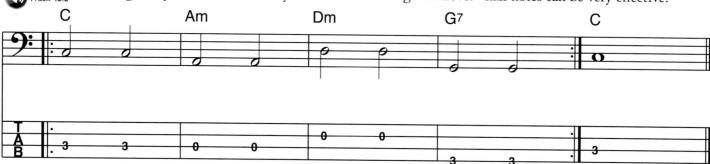

Track 45.3 Many early Motown hits by The Supremes and other groups featured bass lines in quarter notes, all on the root. Play this with a strong rhythmic drive.

Track 45.4 This example should be played at a fairly bright tempo. It mixes various rhythms, but only uses roots.

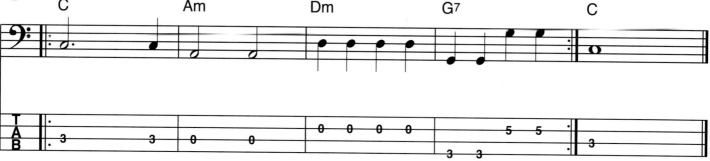

PLAYING FROM CHORD SHEETS (continued)

Many rock hits have been made by picking a catchy rhythm and repeating it throughout the song. Here are some examples of this technique, still limiting ourselves to playing roots.

The dotted quarter/8th note rhythm is characteristic of many rock styles:

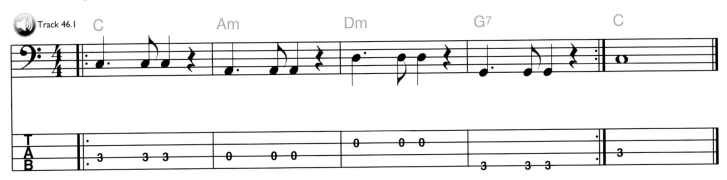

A variation on the above:

A typical syncopated bass figure:

A more complicated syncopation:

PLAYING FROM CHORD SHEETS, Part 2

Now that you know how to construct bass lines using roots, here are some chord progressions in other keys. Make up your own bass lines, patterning them after those of pages 56 & 57.

A really fun way to try out new bass lines is to get a guitar or keyboard player to play the chord progressions along with you.

THE 8TH REST

This symbol stands for 1/2 beat of silence. You can think of it as an unplayed 8th note.

First play measure 1, straight 8th notes. Then play the variations on it, substituting a 1/2 beat of silence for each ♪. After an open note, place your left hand fingers on the string to stop its vibration. After a fingered note, release the pressure on the string but keep the fingers in contact with it to stop its vibration.

Track 48.1

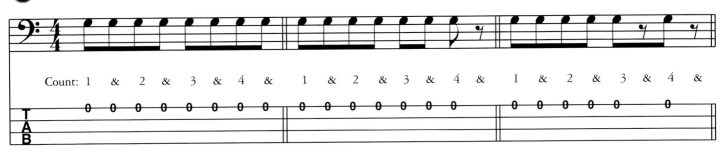

Track 48.2

Track 48.3

Notes Above High C, Part 3

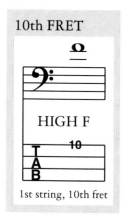

10th FRET

HIGH F

1st string, 10th fret

Knowledge of the high F allows you to extend your range to a full 2-octave scale in the key of F.

Fingering will depend on what precedes and follows the F.

The Two-Octave F Major Scale Track 49.1

Study with High F Track 49.2

* The sign ⁒ is called a repeat sign. It means to repeat the previous measure note for note. Thus, in the example above, the first measure is played a total of three times. Although the repeat sign is rarely seen in printed music, it is very common in hand written manuscripts, so every musician should be familiar with it.

BASS LINES IN F MAJOR

Track 50.1

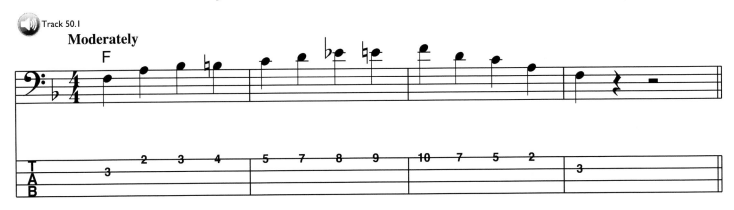

Track 50.2

Track 50.3

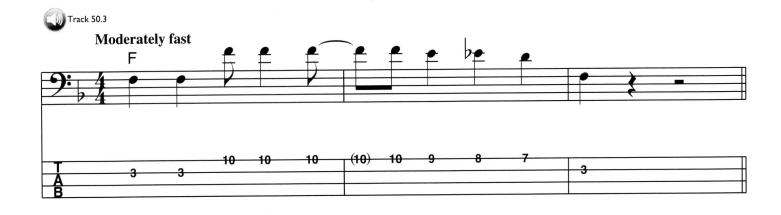

Track 50.4

PLAYING FROM CHORD SHEETS, Part 3

Here are some typical figures based on common chord progressions. The figures make use of the root, 3rd and 5th of each chord, but notice that the root always has the most prominent place in the measure, the first beat.

Analyze each figure, this means that you should understand when you are playing the root, 3rd or 5th. In this way you can adapt these figures to any chord.

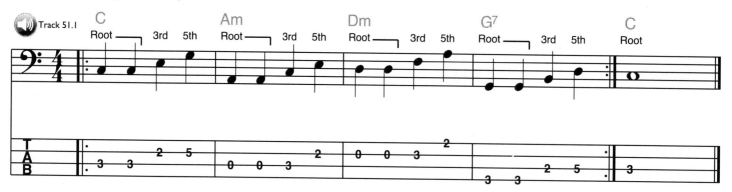

Here is a great figure that was used on the rock classic "In the Midnight Hour."

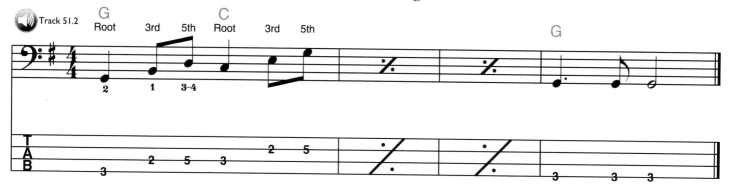

Any chord tone can be approached by a *lower neighbor* note (LN) a half step (one fret) below.

Any chord tone can be approached by an *upper neighbor* note (UN) a half or whole step (one or two frets) above.

PLAYING FROM CHORD SHEETS, Part 4

The I VI IV V Progression

Sometimes Roman numerals are used to refer to chords instead of symbols. The Roman numeral tells you the scale step that the chord is built on. For example, in the key of C, the I chord is a C chord (because the first note in the C scale is a C). In the key of F, the I chord is an F chord; in the key of D, the I chord is a D chord and so on.

The VI chord is a *minor* chord built on the sixth scale step. For example, the VI in C is an A minor chord.

The IV chord is a *major* chord built on the fourth scale step. For example, in the key of C, the IV chord is an F major chord.

The V chord is a *major* chord built on the fifth scale step. For example, in the key of B♭, the V chord is an F major chord.

This chart will show you the I VI IV V chords in all the commonly used keys:

Key	I Chord	VI Chord	IV Chord	V Chord
E	E	C♯m	A	B
A	A	F♯m	D	E
D	D	Bm	G	A
G	G	Em	C	D
C	C	Am	F	G
F	F	Dm	B♭	C
B♭	B♭	Gm	E♭	F

The I VI IV V progression has been used in thousands of songs from swing to rock. Every bass player should be familiar with this progression.

Using the I VI IV V progressions above, make up your own bass lines. Write out the ones you like the best.

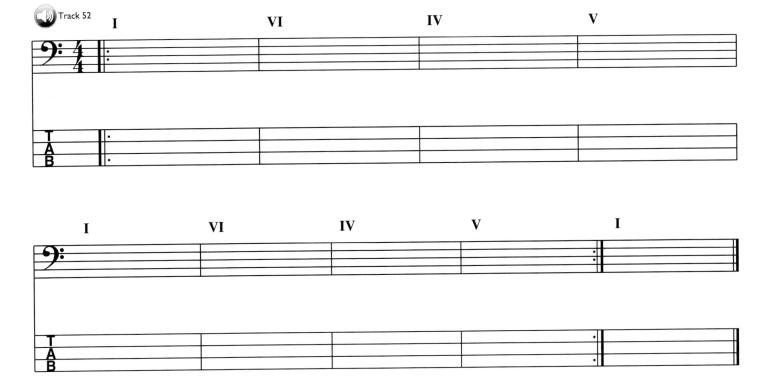

Notes Above High C, Part 4

The final two high notes in this book are F♯ and G. The G note above high C is a very important note, as it lies an *octave* above the open G string. The word *octave* is from the Italian word for eight, and means the eighth note above the one you start with. On the G string, these notes are G, A, B, C, D, E, F♯ and G. All bass guitars have the octave marked in some distinctive way, usually with a double mother-of-pearl dot or diamond shape. The octave is at the 12th fret, and it may be easier for you to find that note and count backwards, back down the fingerboard.

Knowledge of the high F♯ and G notes allows you to play a full two-octave G scale.

11th FRET

HIGH F♯

1st string, 11th fret

12th FRET

HIGH G

1st string, 12th fret

The G Scale in Two Octaves.

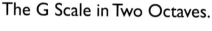

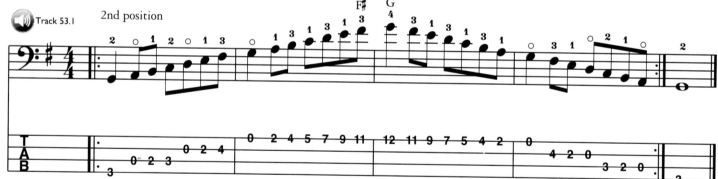

This exercise, called a *chromatic scale*, uses every note in the first octave of the G string.

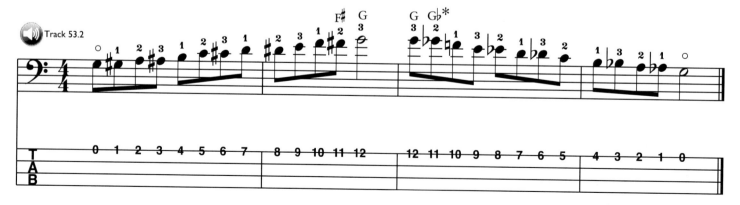

*It is customary when writing out the chromatic scale to use sharps ascending and flats descending.

LICKS AND EXERCISES IN G MAJOR

Track 54.1

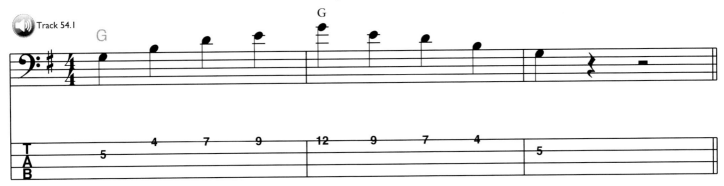

Track 54.2

G Major Exercise with High F# and G

Track 54.3

PLAYING FROM CHORD SHEETS, Part 5

The 12-bar blues progression is rooted in African-American work songs from over one hundred years ago. It has been used for thousands of songs from the earliest printed blues (St. Louis Blues, 1914) to '50s rock songs like "Hound Dog," "Johnny B. Goode" to up-to-date hits by The Black Crowes and other artists that play that good old rock and roll.

Blues are almost always played in major keys, and follow this basic pattern (each Roman numeral stands for one measure):

I I (or IV7) I I7 IV(7) IV(7) I I V7 IV7 I I (or V7 to repeat)

The following examples show you blues progressions in all the most commonly used keys:

On the next page you'll find an example of a B♭ blues with one possible bass line. Our space is too limited to give more examples than this, but the serious student should work out patterns to play in all the above keys.

Also, the blues progressions you've learned are very basic. As shown, they are perfectly adequate for rock and country, but you should be aware that jazz players prefer many sophisticated chords and you may need to look beyond this book for further study.

Blues in B♭

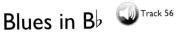 Track 56

Moderately fast

ROCK AND ROLL LICKS FROM THE 1950s

Track 57.1

Track 57.2

Track 57.3

Track 57.4

THE 1960s

'60s Rock Licks

Track 59.1

Track 59.2

'60s Funk Licks

Track 59.3

Track 59.4

Track 60.1

Track 60.2

Track 60.3

Track 60.4

THE 1970s

Track 61.1

Track 61.2

Track 61.3

Track 61.4

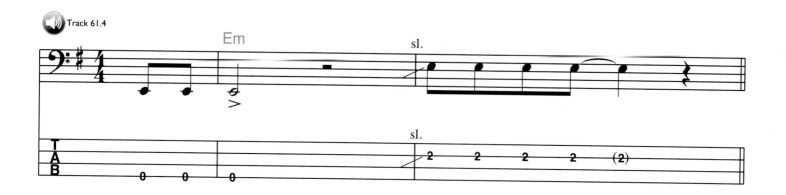

THE 1980s

Track 63.1

Track 63.2

Track 63.3

Track 63.4

THE 1990s

Track 65.1

Track 65.2

Track 65.3

Track 65.4

Track 66.1

Track 66.2

Track 66.3

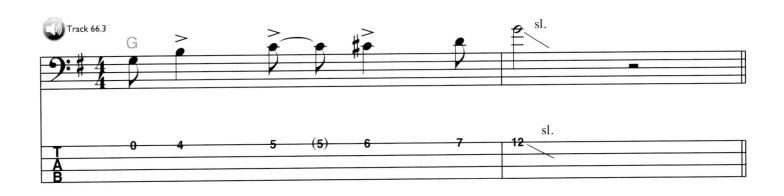

Track 66.4

Bass Guitar Fingerboard Chart

The Bass Notes in the First Octave

The following chart shows the position of every bass note in the first octave, that is, the first twelve frets. This includes every note used in this book as well as those used in the upper positions on the D, A, and E strings

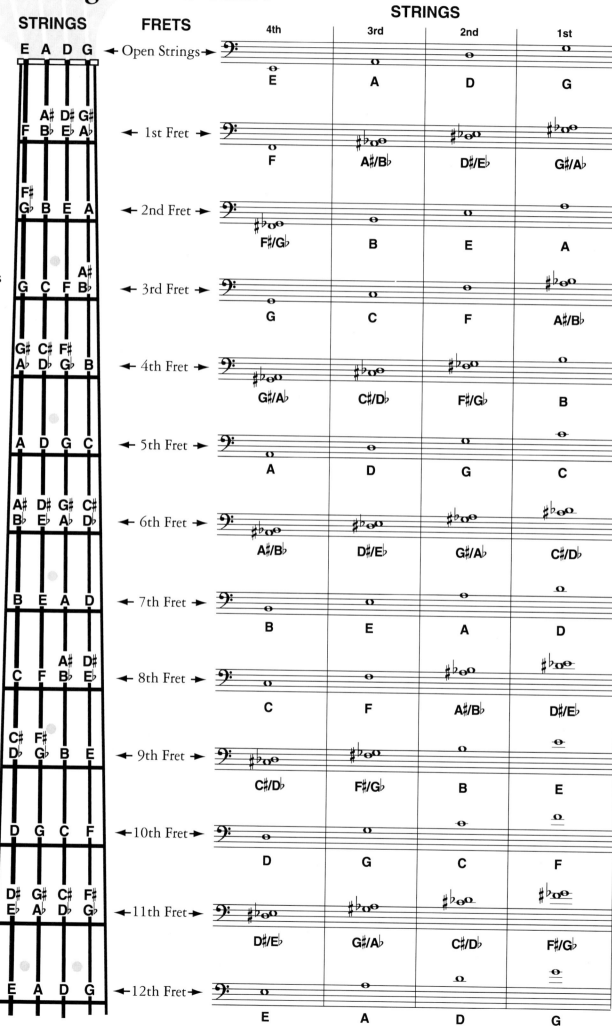

COMPLETE CHORD CHART

The chart below shows how to spell every chord you're ever likely to run across. It inlcudes such keys as Eb, Ab, Db, B and thers that are not often used but still sould be understood by anyone who wants to play professionally.

Also included are the sophisticated chords that modern jazz players like, such as 9ths, 11ths, 13ths, and various altered chords.

The X stands for any chord name.

Root	3rd	5th	6th	Dominant 7th	Major 7th	9th	11th	13th
Ab	C	Eb	F	Gb	G	Bb	Db	F
A	C#	E	F#	G	G#	B	D	F#
Bb	D	F	G	Ab	A	C	Eb	G
B	D#	F#	G#	A	A#	C#	E	G#
C	E	G	A	Bb	B	D	F	A
C#	E	G#	A#	B	B#	D#	F#	A#
Db	F	Ab	Bb	Cb	C	Eb	Gb	Bb
D	F#	A	B	C	C#	E	G	B
Eb	G	Bb	C	Db	D	F	Ab	C
E	G#	B	C#	D	D#	F#	A	C#
F	A	C	D	Eb	E	G	Bb	D
F#	A#	C#	D#	E	E#	G#	B	D#
Gb	Bb	Db	Eb	Fb	F	Ab	Cb	Eb
G	B	D	E	F	F#	A	C	E

NAME OF CHORD	SYMBOL(S)	SPELLING		
Major Triad	X	Root	3rd	5th
Minor Triad	Xm, Xmin., Xmi.	Root	b3rd	5th
Diminished Triad	Xdim.	Root	b3rd	b5th
Augmented Triad	X+, Xaug.	Root	3rd	#5th
Suspended 4th	Xsus4	Root	4th	5th

NAME OF CHORD	SYMBOL(S)				
Major 7th	XM7, Xmaj.7	Root	3rd	5th	7th
Dominant 7th	X7	Root	3rd	5th	b7th
Major 6th	X6, Xmaj.6	Root	3rd	5th	6th
Minor Major 7th	Xmin.maj.7, Xm+7	Root	b3rd	5th	7th
Minor 7th	Xm7, Xmin.7	Root	b3rd	5th	b7th
Minor 6th	Xm6, Xmin.6	Root	b3rd	5th	6th
Diminished 7th	X°7, X°	Root	b3rd	b5th	6th
½ Diminished 7th	X∅7	Root	b3rd	b5th	b7th

Major 7#5, Dominant 7b5, Min.7b5, Maj7#5 etc., are self-explanatory. NOTE: the sign ° indicates diminished seventh, even when the seventh is not mentioned.

NAME OF CHORD	SYMBOL(S)						
Major 9th	Xmaj.9	Root	3rd	5th	7th	9th	9th
Dominant 9th	X9	Root	3rd	5th	b7th	9th	9th
Minor 9th	Xm9, Xmin.9	Root	b3rd	5th	b7th	9th	9th
Diminished 9th	X∅9	Root	b3rd	b5th	6th	9th	9th
Six-Ninth	X⁶⁄₉, X⁶₉	Root	3rd	5th	6th	9th	9th
Minor Six-Ninth	Xmin.⁶₉	Root	b3rd	5th	6th	9th	9th
Augmented 11th	Xaug.11, X#11	Root	3rd	5th	b7th	9th	#11th
Dominant 13th	X13	Root	3rd	5th	b7th	9th	13th

ALL OTHER CHORDS USED ARE ALTERATIONS OF THESE:
C7b9 = C dominant 7th chord plus Db = C-E-G-Bb-Db
G7#5b9 = G dominant 7th chord plus #5 and b9 = G-B-D#-F-Ab
sus4 always means raise the 3rd ½ step: Csus4 = C-F-G

Here is an extra page so you can write out your own bass lines or ones that you hear that you particularly like.